# Top

# Notch

# Tactic's

Written by:

Ronnie Reed & David Guinn

What is success?

Well, that depends on who you ask. Because no one can determine what success is for someone else, simply due to each of us being different in our opinions, goals, and expectations. Therefore what's considered a success for one may not be looked at as the same in the eyes of another.

The best way to define success is... Achieving what one wishes to accomplish.

Now with any level of success, you have to work in order to receive.

## Top-Notch Tactics (TNT)

Imagine you had nothing, or as some say imagine yourself at the bottom of the barrel. You have no money, possess no value possessions, and have no one to call on. Truth be told, you have no idea where your next meal will come from or how you will make it until tomorrow. For some, this is a feeling they couldn't imagine, but for others this is a feeling they know too well. Only because it's their reality.

Now imagine you had everything you wanted in life. Better yet take time to place yourself on top of the world and money is no object, your possessions are the best money can buy and people can't wait for you to call on them, if you ever choose to. Your next meal is from a five star restaurant that you can't even pronounce the name of. And tomorrow is a day that will bring about more success.

I know a lot of people question, is this really possible?

Absolutely!

Top-Notch Tactics is a straightforward, unrestricted way to help ensure your success. Its methods will set you aside from those who use conventional thinking trying to gain above-average status. When successfully utilizing these tactics, one has no choice but to prosper. Let's just say getting what you want and deserve will be inevitable. The key to using these tactics is simply not wavering. Follow the steps as though your life depends on it, because in actuality it does!

Now, here are a few reasons a person's might not use top-notch tactics.

Some think they can never build success with tactics so simple.

Some are afraid they will be ridiculed.

Some simply dream of having the life they want but do nothing to achieve it.

Some start with these tactics but give up they don't see immediate changes within days or if they're faced with adversities.

These tactics work only if you use them, but you must follow the rules. Stick with TNT and don't give up.

Remember nothing in life is an overnight success. Well... maybe the lottery. But what are your chances of hitting that? 1 out of 100 million. With TNT you can make yourself successful by reading it one time and living by its instructions. Never be afraid to go after what you want. After all it's what you want. Plus, you would work harder for yourself than for someone else. If you were to purchase a home would it be a shack or mansion? I'll answer that for you. A mansion. No one in their right mind would buy a shack if they had mansion money.

If you bought a car to compliment your new home, would it be a Kia or Mercedes? Once again, I'll help you out. Mercedes.

Now if your new Mercedes needed gas would you fill it up with regular or Supreme?

Yeah you said it... (Supreme).

Why?

Because you only want what's best for yourself. News Flash! If you don't want the best, then what you want is limited.

Here's something to think about. As of right now before you chose to read TNT you are simply adding to your success. Once you finish reading TNT you'll be multiplying your success.

5+5+5+5+5=25: This is conventional thinking.

5×5=25: This is top-notch thinking.

Surely you noticed a difference in the amplifications. This could be the difference in your success.

Top-Notch Tactics

Top = The highest point.

Notch=score or achieve.

Tactics = An action or strategy carefully planned to achieve a specific end.

## Objects and perspectives

Guard the development of your mission. It doesn't matter if it's personal, financial, or nature. And know that the mind is the only tool needed in life to build and destroy. The life that you were given was not by accident. Just know that you have to discover your living purpose. The concepts of many minds are to get rich, have kids, and a beautiful family. But the question is, how do you get to that success of becoming rich and worry-free. It doesn't just happen! Many have walked the globe and prayed but didn't put in the effort to make their prayer birth itself. The mind works the same way. Some of the outcomes you have in life stem from the thoughts you put in your mind. Does eating a meal sound like a complete visual of the concept I'm showing? You must diet the mind as you do the body. The mind is the most precious creation. However, you would not discover success if you don't have the discipline to control your thinking. Thinking is a tool that the mind used to obtain and retain thoughts that help us discover desires. Once the mind become conscious of the thoughts that it has been processing, we begin to build from within and attract from without. Thoughts are the force with which we build, therefore thoughts are forces. And the degree that thoughts are spiritualized, does it become more subtle and powerful in it's working? I must say yes. The spiritualizing is in accordance with law and it is within the power of all. Everything is first worked out in the unseen before it's manifested in the seen. It's an idea before it is realize in the real. In the spiritual before it is show forth in material. The realm of the unseen is the realm of cause. The realm of the seen is the realm of affect. And always is determined and condition by the nature of its cause.

If any fault lies in us, then the correction of this unnatural condition lies also in us. It is never necessary to come into such a state if we are awake and remain awake mentally to the light and the powers within us. Our thoughts make us what we are. There and thereafter, our thoughts are often busier by night then by day. For when we are asleep to the exterior we can be wide-awake to the interior world. Therefore, the unseen world is a substantial place. The conditions of which are entirely regulated by mental and moral attainments. When we are not driving information through outward avenues of sensation, we are receiving instruction through interior channels of perception. Once this fact is understood for what it is worth, it will become a universal custom for people to take to sleep with them the special subject on which they most earnestly desire particular instruction. It is quite possible to possess a reality that cannot be seen, touched or comprehend it by any of the outer senses. It is faith when we are fully conscious of things not seen, and have the assurance of things not yet manifest. In other words; faith is that consciousness in us, of the reality of the invisible substance and of the attributes of mind by which we lay hold of it. We must realize the mind makes things real according to being birthed into the world from the mother's womb. The babies mind is the Paris of the living life, until the babies mind discovers what emotions are. I will give you a small scenario based on life, living and the way the mind works. When we were children we didn't know how to control our mind. We seemed to always be doing something we didn't have any business in.  This is the point of no return. That will be the true discoveries of the vital realization of our oneness. Some will call this seeing the light. The only reason we stayed into the things we were always told to stay out of is because of the wondering mind.  Seeing the light is not only an understood statement of wisdom. It's the definition of complete mind control. Dream of the objects, and keep your perspective aligned with your objectives, and the building and destroying stages will be like seeing success in 3-D.

# Chapter2

Where you're going, is not as important as how you got there.

In an effort to get here, you have to eliminate catering to emotions, simply because it will stagnant the mental process on moving forward to achieve. Being able to achieve starts with ambition, which stems from desire. Desire is not just a feeling. The feeling is born from the infinite intelligence that is stored in the subconscious mind. The subconscious mind is not the mind we as humans use every day consciously. In order to get to where you are going you have to travel. Along the traveling journey there will be obstacles that will raise brows on how to deal with them, as well as figuring the reason they were presented. Due to immanent abilities we possess, that gives us the assurance of thinking our way out of problems. The mind is the only vessel the human really have no control over. Consciously you can hold your breath as long as your mind tells you to hold it, no matter how long you plan on it. I say that... to say the mind control itself.  The only battle the mind has is with the subconscious. The subconscious is the gear which makes the mind work. It helps us figure, decide and estimate the proper mentality to produce.  When we as humans sit and plan success and don't see it, we worry. Worrying is the emotion that creates the negative energy we need to stay away from. This energy stagnates the mind to think the science of success. There

were many people before you and I
who achieved success through
visualization, before there was the
physical blessing. Our limbic system
instantly transforms thoughts into
physical action as well as symptoms
that make us crave for success. If you
don't have the heart to manage the
success you will never see it in the
physical. The man that created the
airplane did it just come up with a
complete concept overnight or in a
couple of months. Throughout the
planning and building stages there
was failure and it allowed other ideas
to sit in to help the original thought
generate. The proper formula to make
it worth trying over and over is simply
because of the visualization stages.
They saw the plane flying; is the
motivation that kept them searching

for the tools in their mind to help them retrieve the success they searched for. The Wright Brothers were smart men. Again, as a member of their audience I appreciate them for giving us the strength to use the visualization stages to retain success. Dream big! The road that is paved in every humans life is one that is laid by the upbringing in most scenarios. There are a lot of us, who as teenagers, became curious in our life, and thought we were grown at preteen stages in life and have experienced a whole life. But once you became disciplined by an authority figure that trains and teaches on how to use the mind we begin to plan. Without the proper planning and preparing, performing the plan will always be failure. The format that the assassins use are similar to those the mine do naturally. Train the mind. Once we hit the rough patch we want better. The only way to have better is to start thinking consistently. First plan, then prepare. How many men and women look back to our teen years and wish we could've harnessed the ambition instead of hitting the rough patches? To distinguish that there was something within you urging you on to bigger and better things giving you no peace, no rest and no chance to be lazy. Before we realize we possess these powers they fall into the area of the mind that stores doubt. When we go through things along the journey to success, it is the rub that caress the genie of the brain which is the subconscious mind. Suppose you haven't had disappointments and disillusionments along the way. Suppose the fine point of your ambition has become blunted. Remember there is not an obstacle that there is no way around, over or through. And if you doubt the plan you have to overcome the present obstacle there is no complete visualization in your pattern of thinking.

**Fine quote... Mr. Napoleon Hill stated in a book of writings: "fortunate is the person who has developed the self-control to steer a straight course toward his or her objective in life without being swayed from their purpose by either commendation or condemnation."

Know that there will always be a presentation that the mind presents to eliminate the doubt. It all starts with you and the self-disciplined mind and a synchronized heart in order to stay loyal to the thoughts that the subconscious mind feeds the conscious mind. All cause is in the mind; and mind is everywhere, all the knowledge there is, all the wisdom there is and all the power there is. It's all about you no matter where you may be. Your mind is part of it, and you have all the access to it. If you fail to avail yourself of it, you have no one to blame but yourself. Faith is the begotten of a complete understanding. Faith is the impulsion; and the population of this power that propels the subconscious. Faith is confidence and the assurance as well as the enforcing truth that gives us the knowing that the right idea of life will bring you into reality of existence and the manifestation of all the power that one human possesses. Again, all success starts in the mind. You can obtain from the mind anything you want, if you learn how to do it. I think we can rest assured, that one can do and be practically what he or she desires to be.

Psychologists all around the world have similar theories. It is not will power, but desire that rules the world. I have had plenty of desires all my life. I've always wanted to be rich. How do I account for the difference between my wealth, my position, my power, and those of rich men and women all around me? The answer is simply. I have never focused my desires into one great dominating desire.

You madly vision you were rich, and you wish you had a position of responsibility and influence. You wish you could travel at will. Three wishes are so many, yet they conflict with each other and you get nowhere in particular because you lack intense desire. The accomplishment of which you are willing to subordinate everything else. Therefore, figuring out where you are going is the process of figuring yourself out without battling inner mental manipulations. Don't try to do something different that has been designed through desire. Life plays no favorites. Many people habitually set up mental resistance to the flow of life and die or become incarcerated. We don't search for it but by accessing and reproaching gives no one in the world the power to deflect you from your goal. I know where I'm going do you!

Key note: Know the importance in your destination through desire and identify yourself by being loyal to you, first with consistency.

# Chapter 3

Forms of Suggestions

*Auto suggestion

The term autosuggestion means suggesting something definite and specific to oneself. Like any 2 used wrongly it could cause harm, but use properly it can be extremely helpful.

Develop a definite plan for turning over your request or desires to your subconscious mind. Never say, I can't. Overcome that fear by substituting on the following. I can do all things through the power of my subconscious mind and auto suggestion.

*Hetero suggestions

The term his hetero suggestion means suggestions from another person. And all ages, and in every part of the world, the power of suggestion has played a dominant part in the life and thought of humankind. Political creeds, religious beliefs, and cultural customs all flourish and perpetuate themselves through the power of hetero suggestions. * through someone else.

Suggestions can be used as a tool to discipline and control ourselves. However, it can also be used to take control and command over others who have not been taught to understand the laws of the mind. Why do people search for diamonds in the mines instead of searching for them in the minds? And it's

constructive form it is wonderful and
magnificent. And it's negative aspect
it is one of the most distractive of all
the response patterns of the mind. It's
results can be in enduring patterns of
misery, failure, suffering, sickness and
disastrous.

From the day we are born we are
bombarded with negative suggestions,
not knowing how to counter them, we
unconsciously except them and bring
them to being as our experience here
are some examples of negative
suggestions. We all face them until we
identify: you can't,  you'll never
amount to anything, you must not
you'll fail, I don't have a chance,
you're all wrong, it's no use, it's not
what you know but who you know,
what's the use nobody cares, there's

no point to try so hard, you're too old now, Love is for the birds, I just can't win, things are getting worse and worse, I can't trust a soul By accepting hetero Suggestion of this kind, you collaborate and bringing them to pass. As a check out you are helpless when faced with that suggestion of others who were important to you. You did not know any better. The mind, both conscious and unconscious was a mystery you did not even worry about.  As an adult now, how over you are able to make choices constructive and destructive. You can use constructive alto suggestions, which is a reconditioning therapy to change the impressions made on you in the past. The first step is to make yourself aware of the hetero suggestions that are operating on you. Unexamined;

they can create behavior patterns that cause failure in your personal and social life. Constructive auto suggestion can release you from the mass of negative verbal conditioning that might otherwise distort your life pattern, making the development of good habits difficult or even impossible. Whatever the conscious reasoning mind of a person believes, the subconscious mind will except an act upon.

* Ideas and thoughts to stand on

 Faith first: Matthew 21:22 whatever you pray for in faith, you will receive.

Surah 3:200 Ali-Imran O ye who believe! Preserve in patience and consistency; outdo all others in endurance, be ready, and observe your duty to Allah, in order that ye may succeed.

With this suggestion stages you presents remember faith first.

I said all of this and presented this because I'm going to list nine principles that I stand on.

1) Your subconscious mind controls all the vital processes of our body and knows the answers to all problems.

2) Prior to sleep, turn over a specific request so your subconscious mind and prove its miracle working power to yourself.

3) Whatever you impress on your subconscious mind is express on the screen of space as conditions, experiences, and events. Therefore,

you should carefully watch all ideas and thoughts entertained in your conscious mind.

4) The law of action and reaction is universal. Your thoughts is action, and the reaction is the automatic response of the subconscious mind to your thoughts.

5) All frustrations are doing so I'm still feel desires, desires are forfeited thoughts.

6) The life principal will flow through. Feed your mind with her thoughts of harmony, health, peace and all the functions of your body will become normal.

7) Keep your conscience mind busy with high expectations of the best,

and your subconscious will faithfully reproduce your habitual thinking.

8) Imagine the happy ending or solutions to your problems, and cherish the thrills of accomplishments, and what you imagine and feel will be accepted by your subconscious mind, and it will bring it to pass.

9) You must consciously a firm: I believe that the subconscious they gave me this desire is now for filling it through me. This dissolves all conflict with the two.

Imagine the end desired and feel it's reality. Follow it through and you will get an assured results. Think good and good follows. Think evil and evil follows. You are what you think all day long. Follow your mind and apply your thoughts.

# Chapter 4

Say What You Mean, and Mean What You Say

All I have is my balls, and my word is a famous line the Mr. Al Pacino used in the movie Scarface. The statement alone encouraged people to value their words more, and follow up with what words are used. In today's world the value of words are slowly dying, because people are just saying things to soothe the mind of who they are dealing with, and some people use words and don't know how deep words travel into the mind. Remember you have used the same words, not in the same statements or phrases, but the same vocabularies used in language period. Weather in Spanish or English the words mean the same. Before there were words any definition there were symbols signs and gestures that were used to define who was important and who wasn't. Today people have to define character based off of word play alone. Sometimes people are good at disguising who they are by decorating their language, by saying anything. By your words you should be justified by your words you shall be condemned. A person knowing the power of words become very careful of their conversations. They only have to watch the reaction of their words to know that they do not return void. Through the spoken word, man is continually making laws for himself. The invisible forces are working for man who is always pulling the strings himself though he does not know it.

Owing to the vibratory power of words whatever man voices he begins to attract. After man know the truth, he cannot be too careful of his words. Man's only enemies are within himself, and you are the only person that can control the enemy by sorting your words out yourself so mean what you say, and say what you mean because people will judge you based off of how you use your words whether good or bad, so if you told someone that you were going to do something and didn't do it guesswork how does it look to them... untrustworthy...There is an old saying that man only dare use his words for three purposes to heal, Bless or prosper. What man says of others will be said of him, and what he wishes for another he wishes for himself. The

body may be renewed and
transformed through spoken word
and clear vision. God will produce a
great aura of protection about the one
who saves it and no weapon that is
formed against him shall prosper.  In
other words, love and God will
destroy the enemies within oneself,
therefore, one has no enemies all the
external!  There is peace on earth for
him that cherishes he is or her words.
So say what you mean and mean what
you say....

## Step 1 (Dream Big)

The bigger the dream, the bigger the reality. Everything you do or wants out of life starts with a single thought. Napoleon heel said it best if you can conceive and believe, then you can achieve. Nothing starts without a root and the root to your dreams are your thoughts. Remember when you were an adolescent anger parents or teacher asked you what do you want to be when you grow up? Surely you answered by saying what you thought was the best dream job ever. Now after years of living I ask you, Are you what you wanted to become? Or are you where you thought you would be? If you answered no to either question chances are you lead life as a kid supposed to, therefore I'm sure in the course of living things deviated your thoughts from sticking to your dreams. But now since you have an understanding of life it's time for you to re-create your old dream or continue to push for the dreams you have today. Visualize where you want to be and what you want to accomplish based on your perception you can be as close as you want it to be, and since it's only one thought away it's closer than reaching distance. Always remember why your goals/dreams are important to you. Don't spend time worrying about how you will achieve them because when the time is right you'll be presented with an opportunity to take the next step. So focus only on where you want to lan up. There is a universal force that will pull you towards the accomplishments you wish to achieve. The key to jumpstarting that force is using your imagination. Yes, with a little imagination you can have the things you've always wanted. You must deliberately and intentionally wrap your focus around your desires. While concentrating you must feel expectant of the things you want. Visualize yourself with it and know you're going to obtain it. You are not your mind! Therefore you can control it. Illuminate your distractions so you can focus with the precision of laser tunnel vision.  Laser tunnel vision is when you focus on your primary objective. This will only produce increase effectiveness.

The path to big dreams are the visualization stages that generate the comfort of freedom that the mind possesses itself,  and the constant supply of need it wealth lies in recognizing the powers of your conscious mind as well as your subconscious mind and the creative power of your thoughts or mental image dispensary.

Accept the abundant life in your own mind.  Your mental acceptance and expectancy of wealth has it's own mathematics and mechanics of expression. As you enter into the mood of opulence, all things necessary for the abundant life will come to pass.

** Brain food- let this be your daily affirmation; write it in your heart. I am one with my mind so drained be. I am one with infinite riches of my subconscious mind. It is my right to be rich, happy and successful. Money flows to me freely, copiously and endlessly. I am forever conscious of my true worth. I gave of my talents freely, and I am wonderfully blessed financially. It's wonderful! Apply this method daily with affirmation of dreaming big and be bold enough to claim that it is your right to be rich, and your deeper mind will honor your claim.

**Tactics  to use and plants in the mind to help dream big...

1) Don't make money your sole aim, Claim wealth happiness and peace to for all.

2) Do not make a God of money. It is only a symbol. Remember riches or in

the mind. You are here to lead a balanced life – this includes acquiring all the money you need.

3) You are not here to live in a hotel, to dress in rages, or to go hungry. You are here to lead the life more abundant.

4) Repeat frequently; I like money. I use it wisely, constructively and fruitfully. I release it with joy, and it returns abundantly. Repeat...

5) There is no virtue in poverty. It is a disease of the mind. You should heal yourself of this mental conflict at once.

6) Picture the end result in your mind it causes your subconscious to respond and fulfill your mental picture.

If you give mental attention to your goals, ideas, and enterprises your deeper mind will back you up. The key to wealth is to apply the laws of the subconscious mind by impregnating it with the idea of wealth. Your subconscious multiplies and magnifies whatever you deposit in it. Every morning upon waking deposit thoughts of prosperity, success, wealth and peace. Dwell upon these concepts. Busy the mind with them as often as possible. These constructive thoughts will find their way as deposits in your subconscious mind, and bring forth abundance and prosperity so dream big.

**Brain food-

Imagination is your most powerful faculty. Imagine what is lovely and of

good report. You are what you
imagine yourself to be...So get
money!!!

# Step 2 (Self Confidence)

Being confident in yourself is one of the most essential tactics and working towards accomplishing your dreams. Self-confidence doesn't mean you have to be arrogant, just be assured of yourself and your capabilities. Don't confuse cockiness with confidence because the two are very different. The first is a way people act to boost their self-esteem. The second is simply having faith in yourself, believing you can do it. Confidence is a motivational tool that pushes one towards fulfillment. "Without it there would be no extra effort, determination or fortitude on one's behalf," quote by Ronnie Reed. If you don't believe in yourself then why would others believe in you? Just by being your authentic self will help you gain great success. Always be confident in everything, looks, plans, capabilities etc. By doing so it adds credibility to your reputation and helps you move forward with greater ease. Everyone is attracted to those who know where they are headed. With confidence times influence and the more influence you have the more success you can have. Associates, friends, and family will invest in you and your confidence will be their primary reason.

Self-criticism brings about doubt and all leaders possess confidence. Successful people never doubt themselves. Every time you can produce results or achieve something you gain credibility and confidence to move forward and with each step other people's doubts about you will evaporate.

Confidence is contagious. Just by being around confident people others usually perform better because they believe their expectations are higher and that will help you attract opportunities more easily.

Confidence and certainty will both get you further ahead in the end you will find yourself out performing your own expectations. But first you must be willing to trust your instincts, but knowing and understanding that every result cultivates and develop an aura that attracts people unintentionally. People call you Lucky, that things come your way, that you have come into an understanding of the fundamental laws of nature and have put yourself in harmony with them; and you are in song with infinite; that you understand the law of attraction.

 Confidence is the creative power. It gives you the ability to create for yourself. It does not mean the ability to take from someone else. Confidence develops insight and SAGACITY and increased independence, the ability and disposition to be helpful. It destroys distrust, depression, fear and every form of slacking. Confidence awakens buried talents. It has changed the lives of thousands of men and women once it's aligned. Some people have the ability to be confident, but they allow low self-esteem to set in due to some form of hetero suggestions. So don't allow anyone to steal your vibe.

Confidence teaches principles and suggests methods for making a practical application of the principles; in that it differs from every other course of human studies. It teaches that the only possible value which can attach to any principle and its application. Many read books on how to apply the application.  It isn't applicable, it's based on absolute scientific truth and will unfold the possibilities that lie dormant in the individual, and teach how they may be brought into action. To increase the persons effective capacity, bringing edit energy = (Swaggin) = cultivate and develop an understanding before words are spoken. Confident you have to attain this power, but you have to understand it. You have to use it you have to control it. You want to impregnate yourself with this momentum daily. Go to sleep with it and awake with it. "Right now", you read or if you were not confident where do you think you will be with yourself? I can't answer that question. I've never experienced low self-esteem. Not saying it can't happen, but I refuse to allow that to sit on my brain.

My level of confidence stays on an extreme level so maintain your status and protect your reputation by staying confident...

*Brain food- confidence= the attacks success, power, and wealth attainment, with very little conscious effort so stay swaggin my friend...

## Step 3 (Plan, Plan, Plan)

Everything that has been built
(homes, buildings, careers, brands and
businesses) or is going to be built in

the future has a plan or a blueprint as some call them. What some people call luck or good fortune is really what happens when proper preparation meets up with the perfect opportunity.

Look at it this way, basketball superstar Steph Curry spends countless hours practicing, shooting the ball from half court. So when its 2.2 seconds left in the fourth quarter and his team is down by two points he's only option is to shoot from where he stands half court. Without failure the ball goes in and his team wins by one point. Is this luck? No! It's proper preparation preventing poor performance. If he would've never planned for those types of shots he would've never been ready for the opportunity.  Planning is your pre-meditated step toward success. When you calculate your moves it doesn't mean you won't face trouble times. But you will know the next steps to take if they arrive. Why? Because you'll be prepared. Plans are a course of actions intended to influence and determine decisions. They are your certificates of insurance. In order to master your work don't get stuck in analysis. Simply try and try again.

## Step 4 (Network)

Networking is like the carpool to success! So socialize with those who are headed in the same direction as yourself. And it's always good to know someone who knows someone. Just remember to be honest with yourself about your talent, time and resources. This way you'll know in exactly what areas you could use assistance in or how you can assist someone.

Networking is like the carpool to success! So socialize with those who are headed in the same direction as yourself. And it's always good to know someone who knows someone. Just remember to be honest with yourself about your talent, time and resources. This way you'll know in exactly what areas you could use assistance in or how you could assist someone.

View networking as stated: it's having the key to anything simply because of who you know or who and what they know. For every person you know they know two and so on and so on. It's like having extended arms are longer legs. You could reach higher or get there faster. Contacts, connections and go-betweens are all vital pieces in getting to where you wish to be. There may be some doors or some things you just can't open or do, so you would know someone who can. Networking is a life line. Be true to yourself and allow others a chance to help you by showing common vision with others you will attain some of the greatest success possible and when you do, acknowledge it and appreciate it. Selfish people don't get many chances at success. And how far you get in achieving things will sometimes be determined by the people you spend your time with. Are you familiar with the saying birds of a feather? If so then you know socializing with success breeds success. In order for you to maximize networking resolve any disharmony among its members. It's the only way you can get results. One of the most valuable skills you can have is the ability to communicate effectively with others. Team performance will always have more velocity when organized. Plus you'll learn more, especially if you are a good listener. You should constantly look for windows of opportunity and with networking you'll get chances that otherwise would have been missed. When your success perceives you others will be inclined to present opportunities to you. You risk your success when you Envelop yourself with people whose confidence or at a lower standard than yours. You can easily tell when networking is working for you when business and contacts are attracted to you and you can't identify their source.

## Step5 (Negotiate)

Communicating is the key! Surely you've heard the phrase conversation rules the nation. Well it's true;

nothing is more powerful than words nothing! Now can you believe 72% of conversations that take place between individuals or spent negotiating? Anywhere from trying to get others to see your point of view, down to telling a kid that you'll reward them for being good. Both are a form of negotiation. Whenever you try to change a person's opinion or make a trade off to your liking or benefit you negotiate. In no way does it require manipulation deception or wrong-doings. It's all about understanding and finding the common ground. A fair exchange is no robbery simply because both parties will be satisfied with the outcome. Before you make a proposal wait until the other person tells you what they want and what they can give. They may be willing to give more than you expected. A good negotiator that has an acquired skill for knowing when to move and when to step back. Before encountering any communication first you must carefully evaluate the outcome. You should form strategies to bring about the desired response. Without the strategies you could compromise what you want way before the negotiation starts.

If you really want to be successful in negotiating you must always know what's at stake. By knowing was it steak you can strategize more effectively. Sometimes the best negotiation you can do is walking away. When you gather all the facts and information it will give you a tremendous advantage. In the beginning of any negotiation always ask for more then you need because the other side will try to take you down. In certain cases there will be things that mean nothing to you but could be the most important thing to the other person. So treat everything dearly and never reveal what is important to you in the beginning. Body language and facial expressions are way more telling than words so try to do every negotiation face-to-face. Don't make decisions out of the emotions because if you do they will be rationalized later, but the deal would be done. Plus when people get caught up in negotiating emotionally it's harder for them to walk away. Be sure to create a good reason for the other side to act now.  And always make it seem as though you have options. By doing this you always gain more leverage.

John F Kennedy said it let us never negotiate out of fear, but let us never fear to negotiate. Never settle for anything that comes standard because everything is negotiable. Any astute business person will tell you that negotiation is essential part of closing a deal...

You must be in a position of power to negotiate. First establish rapport in the phases of negotiating by declaring what it is you are looking for in the negotiation. When dealing with people in the negotiation the value of what is being negotiated on must be wanted by both parties first without that being reason there will be no compromise. All too often we get into negotiations with a front man or woman. These people are usually the ones that will try to recite rules and standard practices of their company. If you propose anything different, they will either say no or have you speak to their boss; so therefore skip the yes-man and negotiate with another person of power. Never let someone tell you no when they can tell you yes, and always be confident in yourself and your offer and find creative ways to exchange services as opposed to paying for them. When you go negotiating always remember the other person you negotiate with must be equal to you and possess the same authority.

Function of negotiation questions.

What are the functions of questions in the process of negotiating?

1) (To get someone's attention)

Some questions speak to what people want.

2) (To get information)

This is obviously the most common function of questions. Home?, What?, Why?, When?, How? Knowledge is power in a negotiation. Ask the right questions and answer them the right way, and make sure you listen to details.

3) (Give information)

Do you think anyone would ever ask a question to give information? What does this do? What are we discussing? You should use this type of tactic to give the person you are negotiating with information they do not have.

4) (Buy time)

Sometimes in the process of negotiating we ask questions that will buy us some time to get the edge in making a deal, these sound like information gathering questions but the motive is different. Remember the question must not appear to the other party as a stalling tactic.

5) (Lead or mold thinking)

Quick wittedly asked questions can move the other parties thinking in the direction you wanted to flow in, rather than selling or tilling the vantage of your proposal.

6) (Determine the other party's position)

And a negotiation, there are important questions that can be used to determine where the other party is in the negotiation process (getting info) in your next negotiation weather with your children, your wife or business mate or partners pay particular attention to the amount of time you spend asking questions or demanding.

 Benjamin Franklin once stated remember not only to say the right thing at the right time in the right place but far more difficult still to leave an said the wrong thing at the wrong time. The motivation of willingness to listen does not come naturally to most people. Most would rather talk than listen. Who is the typical thought process. If I can be persuasive in the things I say, I could convince the other party of what is needed to successfully complete a negotiation and satisfy my needs. This is often faulty thinking for three reasons:

1) You are going to waste a lot of time trying to convince the other party.

2) You are assuming that you know what they need to reach an agreement. The assumptions' are usually incomplete

3) You will be so busy thinking about what you were going to say next that you won't concentrate on what the other party is saying. Do as much research as you can before a

negotiation begins. Your best tool is listening that's the reason for two ears.

Listen more than we talk, because if we had to mouth we couldn't listen enough. This is a precise way to keep down conflict or the whining phases of injustice in the stages of a negotiation. If your organization is small in numbers, then do what Gideon did conceal the members in the dark but raise a din and clamor that will make the listener believe that your organization numbers many more than it does.

Power tactic ** Power is not only what you have but what people think you have.

In a negotiation be as deterrent as the mission you have set out to deter is simply a matter of turning this dynamic around, altering any perception of yourself as a week in naïve and sending the message that battle with you would not be as easy as they had thought.  This is generally done by thinking some visible action that will confuse the aggressor and make them think they have miss read you. You may indeed be vulnerable, but they are not sure. You're disguising your weakness and distracting them. Action has much more credibility than mere threatening or fiery words; Heading back for instance, even in some small symbolic way it will show that you mean what you say. I only ask you not to go into a negotiation with the fear of losing. Go into it with the mindset of an assassin. Win**

# Step 6 (Take Chances)

Nothing in life is without risk it just comes with the territory. If you truly wish to be successful then you must abandon the thought of failure and take chances. Sometimes you must do what others wouldn't even consider. Don't be afraid to stand out against conventional thinkers. Those who continue to use the strategies of the past will only get the results of the past. When a person takes risk it shows they have confidence in themselves and their abilities to be fearless in your approach to new opportunities.

Taking chances makes champions. If you don't have the courage to take chances you won't discover the feeling of a champion. If you are an entrepreneur you take chances you just have to be careful in the ones you take. Infidelity is a good example in the visualization of taking chances. We don't intend on cheating we just take the chance of not getting caught, if you're caught there goes the neighborhood; so remain fearless in every approach of taking chances because the wrong one could get looked down upon or it could block your blessings. (Taking chances make champions...) Quote by David Guinn

However desperate to situation and circumstances don't despair. When there is everything to fear, be unafraid, when surrounded by danger fear none of them. The boxer for instance the superior fighter does not rely on his power punch or quick reflexes. Instead he creates a rhythm to the fight that suits him, advancing and retreating at a pace he sets; he controls the ring moving his opponent to the center, to the ropes toward or away from him mastering the art of taking chances he creates frustration, compels mistakes and engenders is a mental collapse that precedes the physical. He wins not with his face but because he took a chance on changing his fighting style. In all things we do in life is based on the right timing and a perfect chance. How would we have discovered electricity if chances weren't taken. People will use any kind of gap in your defenses to attack you or revenge themselves on you. So offer no gaps to allow someone to not take a chance on you; so stay relentless in creating pressure on all sides and remain dominant in seeking attention in maintaining control of the situation. Because taking a chance alone without having a clear motive What's the point in taking a chance… Right? So stay focus on the plan at hand so the precision at taking that chance could be a dominant one. Proper preparation, prevents poor performance this. (Right on!!)

In the story the horns of the beast The Zulu Warriors took a chance fighting the British they took chances and trained in terrain. They had no clue if their enemy would ever be there but amongst preparing for a challenge unlike no other they had no clue if the Swords and shields would be enough for the British. Knowing that their fighting styles are different; simply because he knew taking a knife to a gun fight is crucial to begin with. So again he took chances training in terrain He had no clue if the enemy would ever be there. He and other Zulu Warriors would practice formations with visualization of the enemy being in place, so upon attack they would know how to react. The people didn't only do this one time and it was over. After every battle they would train different not knowing how in a pony would react to their preparation. No preparation was the same as not having a chance. In order to take chances you have to be able to agree with a chance it's self, simply because the chance doesn't want to risk taking a chance on you. So know every step in preparing for taking chances by doing your homework on whatever it is you're willing to invest your energy in and stay humble...

# Step 7 (Be Persistent)

Failure is no option for those who wish to be successful. Why? Because they never give up. They except losses or setbacks and view them as life lessons, using those experiences to rethink, redefine or re-strategize their moves.

Nothing in the world can take the place of persistence. Persistence and determination are omnipotent. The slogan press on has solved and always will solve the problems of the human race. Quoted by Calvin Coolidge. Successful individuals look back up on failure as if it was an opportunity to embark on a new path a rebirth and a time move on.

Never blame circumstances, instead accept responsibility. Recommit to the steps that are necessary to achieve the intended results. Committed people build the foundation to everything that constantly produces the almost impossible results. It's never good to break away from commitments. When you set out to do something then make sure it is done. Your efforts to stay aboard will produce more constant results. And after accomplishments are achieved one becomes prouder. Accept your weaknesses but always work to strengthening them. Work only on solutions. To effectively build success sometimes requires you to go back to complete things you left incomplete. The longer you delay doing what is necessary to become successful the harder it becomes. Don't be frozen by your mistakes, simply detach yourself from failure. Then you will be able to propel new opportunities into action.

# Bracket of Entrepreneurship

This Bracket is the module outline of what it takes to start your path to entrepreneurship.

First you need to know the field of business you wish to be in. And once you have that figured out do your research.

Now let us just fast forward and say that you already know what you want to do you just need the steps on how to get things started.

## Business address

Your business address should always be different from your home address. The reason for this is because your business info will be a public record, which means anyone can look the business up.

If you don't have a business address then no worries, getting one is extremely easy.

You can use a P.O. Box or a virtual office.

I believe that a virtual office is way better than a P.O. Box, especially if you choose to build business credit.

You can obtain a virtual office with a company named True Space or simply google virtual office and numerous listing will appear.

# Register the business name.

There's a few ways to get this done. You can either start off with a DBA (Doing Business As) or LLC (Limited Liability Company)

If you choose to do it as a DBA you need to go to your local county clerk's office to register the name. During this process you will first use their computer to conduct a search to make sure that no one else is using the name that you want. Second you will pay the fee to have the name registered.

The county clerk will provide you with the registration of your business the same day.

Now if you choose to register as an LLC there are plenty of organization to help you do so. One of my favorites is Legal Zoom. Simply go to the Legal Zoom website and check out their packets and payment plans. Once you decide what option you want, it normally takes about 10 business days to receive you LLC credentials in the mail. In this LLC credential packet you should have your EIN (Employer Identification Number), Articles of organization, a seal stamp with your company's name on it and certificates of ownership.

Now you can go to the IRS.gov website and apply for your EIN yourself. And it's FREE, however you won't receive the other things mentioned above that comes with using Legal Zoom.

# How to open a business Bank Account

Once you have the company registered you can take those registration papers to the bank of your choice to open an account.

Before you just open an account here are some things to consider.

1. Do they charge for each deposit? If so, how much?
2. Do they pay interest on business checking accounts? If so, what's the minimum balance required?

3. How often is the interest on the account earned or posted?
4. What's the bank record of giving loans to small businesses?

## Building business credit

There are quite a few things you should do when you're trying to build business credit.

The first thing you should do is get your DUNS number.

Go to the Dun & Bradstreet website. Create your login and register your company with them. They are like the credit bureau for businesses. This is the company that all creditors use when searching your business credit.

Now that you have secured your DUNS number you want to look for creditors.

The best creditors to reach out to are Net 30 creditors. These are companies like Quail, Fuelman, and U-line. Just to name a few.

You can always find more by googling Net 30 creditors.

# Building personal credit

When it comes to building personal credit there are plenty of ways to do that.

Let us say that you already have a personal bank account.

Go to your bank and let them know that you would like to get a secured credit card. Most bank start secured credit cards with a minimum of $300.

What will happen is you give the bank $300 and they will give you a credit card with a $300 limit on it. Use this card to for small purchases, like gas or fast food. Don't use it for anything major.  Once the billing statement comes out, pay the bill monthly. This will reflect on your credit as an open account.

Once you have six months or more paying this bill monthly you should go back to the back and ask them to take the secured off of the credit card. What they will do is give you back the original $300 that you gave them. And you will still have the card with the $300 limit. It will also be beneficial to ask the for a limit increase.

Something else you can do is open up a savings building account.

With a savings building account you simply state how much money you wish to save for one year. So lets say you wish to save $1000 in a year. What you would do is pay yourself $83 a month until you reach the one year mark. Once you have it paid off the bank will give you the money that you have been paying yourself. However each time that you made a payment it was going on your credit, therefore helping you raise your credit score.

You can also create an account with a company named Fingerhut.

Simply go to their website and do so. They normally start a person out with a credit limit of $250.

The name of the game is to get the small credit lines so you can pay them off. Once you pay them off you can always ask for a credit increase. You will also be attracting the attention of other creditors like American Express, Discover, and Capital One.

All of whom will start sending you offers to build credit with them.

This book is dedicated to the memory of David Guinn (9/25/1979 – (7/27/2020)

Ronnie Reed, author of Two Choices, Top Notch Tactic's, and C.H.A.M.P.

He currently is working on other books and a movie.

He's the founder of TILTIT360CRYO, a mobile cryotherapy center, which helps people prevent and recover from injuries.

All inquiries can be sent to: ardpublishing@gmail.com

www.ingramcontent.com/pod-product-compliance
Lightning Source LLC
LaVergne TN
LVHW051151080426
835508LV00021B/2578